W9-BQS-661

HEINEMANN Profiles

Jesse Owens

Endeavour College
PO Box 80 Enfield Plaza
Enfield SA 5085

Philip Steele

Heinemann
LIBRARY

H **www.heinemann.co.uk**
Visit our website to find out more information about **Heinemann Library** books.

To order:
☎ Phone 44 (0) 1865 888066
▤ Send a fax to 44 (0) 1865 314091
▯ Visit the Heinemann Bookshop at www.heinemann.co.uk to browse our catalogue and order online.

First published in Great Britain by Heinemann Library, Halley Court, Jordan Hill, Oxford OX2 8EJ, a division of Reed Educational and Professional Publishing Ltd.
Heinemann is a registered trademark of Reed Educational & Professional Publishing Limited.

OXFORD MELBOURNE AUCKLAND JOHANNESBURG BLANTYRE GABORONE IBADAN PORTSMOUTH NH (USA) CHICAGO

Produced for Heinemann Library by Discovery Books Limited
Edited by Patience Coster
Designed by Ian Winton
Originated by Dot Gradations
Printed and bound in Hong Kong/China

ISBN 0 431 08646 X (hardback)
05 04 03 02 01
10 9 8 7 6 5 4 3 2 1

British Library Cataloguing in Publication Data

Steele, Philip
Jesse Owens. – (Heinemann Profiles)
1. Owens, Jesse, 1913-1980 – Juvenile literature 2. Olympic Games (11th) : – Juvenile literature 3. Track and field athletes – United States – Biography – Juvenile literature 4. Afro-American athletes – United States – Biography – Juvenile Literature
I. Title
796.4'2'092

Acknowledgements
The Publishers would like to thank the following for permission to reproduce photographs:
Bettman/Corbis pp10, 15, 16, 17, 19, 21, 22, 27, 34, 35, 38, 39, 40, 42, 44; Cleveland Press Collection/ Cleveland State University Library pp12, 20; Corbis pp8, 45, 51; Hulton Deutsch Collection p14; Hulton Deutsch Collection/Corbis pp25, 26; Hulton Getty pp5, 9; Hulton Getty/Allsport p28; Keystone/Hulton Getty p37; Peter Newark's Military Pictures p24; Popperfoto pp29, 30, 31, 32, 33, 46, 48, 49.

Cover photograph reproduced with permission of Hulton Getty

Every effort has been made to contact copyright holders of any material reproduced in this book. Any omissions will be rectified in subsequent printings if notice is given to the Publisher.

Any words appearing in the text in bold, **like this**, are explained in the Glossary.

CONTENTS

WHO WAS JESSE OWENS?

It is August, 1936. In the fashionable streets and beer gardens of Berlin everybody is talking about one subject – the **Olympic Games**. This ancient festival of athletics, revived in 1896, is held every four years. It is about to be staged in the German capital and it promises to be the biggest and most modern sporting event the world has ever seen.

THE GAMES OF HATE?

Germany is ruled by the National Socialist German Workers' Party, known in short as the **Nazis**. Their **swastika** badge, a crooked black cross, appears on red and white flags which flutter everywhere. The Nazi leader is Adolf Hitler (1889-1945), a ruthless and cunning politician. He has a burning hatred of peoples he dismisses as inferior – Jews, Blacks, Slavs and Gypsies.

As Hitler steps out of his open-topped car to enter the Olympic stadium, a great roar goes up. Thousands of voices shout 'Heil Hitler!' ('Hail Hitler!') and a forest of arms is raised into the air, as the crowd makes the Nazi salute.

To the athletes who have gathered here from all over the world to take part in the games, it is a chilling sound. Some of them belong to those

ethnic groups despised by the Nazis. One of the athletes is a wiry, mild-mannered, charming African-American. His name is Jesse Owens.

RUNNING FOR FREEDOM

Jesse Owens was one of the greatest sportsmen the world has ever seen. He was a natural athlete, running and jumping with matchless speed and grace. Jesse lived through a century of war and political violence. He was constantly buffeted by the tide of great events beyond his control. He endured a poverty-stricken childhood and faced **racism** at home as well as abroad. Today he is remembered with affection and admiration by African-Americans and by countless other people all over the world, because at the Berlin Olympics that August in 1936, against great odds, Jesse Owens made history.

Jesse Owens displays perfect style at the Berlin Olympics.

AN ALABAMA CHILDHOOD

Jesse was born far from Berlin, in Oakville, Alabama, in the southern United States on 12 September 1913. His parents, Henry and Emma, gave him the name James Cleveland Owens.

BLACK AND WHITE

At that time, Alabama had a population of over two million people. About forty-three per cent of the people were of African-American descent, and most of the remainder were of European descent. Jesse's grandparents had been born as **slaves**. Slavery was only abolished in the United States in 1865, after a bitter **civil war**.

What is racism?

Many people used to believe that human beings could be divided into groups called 'races' according to their physical appearance. They placed great emphasis on minor physical differences between **ethnic groups**.

Racists not only believe that racial divisions are important, but that some races are superior to others. In the 1920s and 1930s, racist ideas were commonplace among white people all over the world.

However, following advances in the study of **genetics**, most scientists now believe that such divisions are simply not meaningful. The genetic differences between the ethnic groups are very small. It makes much more sense to say that there is only one 'race' – the human race.

By the time Jesse was born, African-Americans had their freedom, but especially in the southern states, society remained **segregated**, or divided. This meant that African-Americans were not treated equally with their white neighbours. Schools were also segregated, and black children like Jesse were given few chances in life.

LIVING OFF THE LAND

In the 1900s, eighty-three per cent of people in Alabama were country dwellers. The chief crop in the region was cotton, which grows well in the hot summer sunshine of the south. However, since 1909, many Alabama farmers had become fearful for their livelihood, because a destructive pest called the boll weevil had crossed into their state from Mississippi, and it threatened the cotton crop. Like most of his neighbours, Henry Owens was a **sharecropper**, a kind of tenant farmer. His small, timber house was the property of the landlord, and rent was paid in the form of a large share of the crop. The family had to survive on the money brought in by the remainder of the share. It was a hard life, and Jesse was the youngest of ten children, with three sisters and six brothers. He was a rather sickly boy who suffered several times from **pneumonia** and bronchial congestion. There was no money to buy medicine and his parents had to nurse him through several bouts of illness.

OFF TO SCHOOL

Jesse's mother, Emma, was determined that her children would make a success of their lives, despite all the problems. At the age of six, Jesse went to school. In those days there were no school buses, and Jesse faced a very long walk to the little school, which was a simple hut used as a Baptist chapel on Sundays. He soon learned to read and write.

Blacks in the American south faced poverty and racism. However, shared problems bred strong community values and family bonds.

In the spring and autumn, there was so much work to do on the land that the children of the **sharecroppers** had to help out in the fields rather than go to school. It was tough, back-breaking work under a blazing sun. There was little machinery on farms at that time, just muscle power. Mules were still widely used for ploughing the land in the southern states.

Sharecroppers worked hard but received a meagre share of the profits.

GAMES AND RUNNING

However it was not all hard work and Jesse would later remember his early childhood as a happy one. Jesse loved to swim and play outdoors with his friends. Even then, it was clear that he was a fast runner – just as his father had been in his day. He loved running for the sense of freedom it gave him as he explored the Alabama countryside. But his days as a country boy were coming to an end.

'I always loved running…. You could go in any direction, fast or slow as you wanted, fighting the wind if you felt like it… '
Jesse Owens, on his childhood

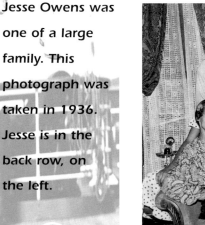

'JC'

When Jesse was aged nine, the Owens family made a big decision. The idea first came from Jesse's sister Lillie, who had moved to Cleveland, Ohio. She wrote to tell them that this northern city was the place to get ahead in life, somewhere to leave the poverty of the **sharecropping** life far behind.

Henry Owens was all too aware that his skills as a farmer would be of little use in the big city, but Emma persuaded him that it really was time for a change. They had nothing to lose. With mixed feelings, the Owens family headed north by train, bound for Cleveland's East Side.

CITY OF STEEL

Cleveland was a sprawling industrial city, built where the Cuyahoga River flows into Lake Erie. One reason for its success was that it provided a link

Jesse Owens was one of a large family. This photograph was taken in 1936. Jesse is in the back row, on the left.

between the iron ore-producing regions around Lake Superior and the coal mines of Ohio, Pennsylvania and West Virginia.

Industry in Cleveland centred around steel manufacture. Henry and Jesse's older brothers found work in the steel mills. Emma worked hard cleaning houses and taking in laundry.

Cleveland was a rapidly growing city which had attracted many **immigrants** from other parts of the world. Its population included Irish, Germans, Italians, Jews, Central Europeans, and many African-Americans escaping the southern countryside, just like the Owens family.

Jesse soon learned one difference between Ohio and Alabama. The **elementary school** to which he would be sent was **integrated**. It took both black and white pupils.

'JC' BECOMES JESSE

It was at elementary school that Jesse was first called 'Jesse'. At birth he had been given the names James Cleveland Owens, but most people called him 'JC' for short. When he hesitantly told his new teacher that he was called 'JC', she misunderstood and registered him as 'Jesse' Owens. The name would stick for the rest of his life.

Part-time jobs

Jesse soon settled down in his new home, although he still suffered from bouts of illness. He helped to bring in some money too by doing all kinds of part-time jobs. He delivered groceries and helped out at a shoe-repair shop.

Riley to the rescue

Jesse Owens and coach Charles Riley soon developed a strong respect for each other.

It was when Jesse moved up to Fairmount Junior High School that he began to make his mark – as an athlete. The man who first spotted his talent was a square-jawed, bespectacled Irish-American called Charles Riley, who was athletics coach at Fairmount. The two got on very well and Jesse called him 'Pop'.

Riley, often in shirt-sleeves, flat cap and bow tie, was always out on the track with the teenager. Riley made Jesse run, run and run some more. He made Jesse try out the 440 yards (402 metres) and the 100 yards (91 metres) sprint. He introduced him to hurdles, long jump and high jump. The boy became stronger and fitter. Riley encouraged the relaxed, natural style of running that was to become Jesse's trademark.

> 'I got up with the sun, ate my breakfast even before my mother and sister and brothers, and went to school, winter, spring and fall alike, to run and jump and bend my body this way and that... '
>
> Jesse Owens, on training

In 1928 Riley introduced Jesse to an athlete called Charlie Paddock, a gold medallist at the 1920 **Olympic Games**. Jesse was inspired. He could already run 100 yards in 11 seconds. He was selected for the Fairmount track team. He became determined to be a great athlete too, one day.

In 1929, a car hit Jesse's father, breaking his leg. He was off work and then lost his job at the steel mill. Henry Owens' chance of finding new work was slim. His eyesight was failing. What was more, in that same year the US **economy** crashed. In the years that followed, in the United States and around the world, more and more people became unemployed and many suffered great hardship during the period called the Great Depression.

Jesse's family made a wise choice. Jesse should not quit his schooling now, in order to bring in more money. In the long term, they decided, it would be better for him to stay on and finish his education.

A RISING STAR

Jesse Owens,
aged 19,
represents
Cleveland's East
Technical High
School in 1932.

Jesse Owens was growing up. He was popular, good fun, a sharp dresser – and hard-working, too. One of his best friends at Fairmount Junior High School was an attractive, lively teenager called Minnie Ruth Solomon. She too was African-American and from a very similar background to Jesse. The two young people were immediately attracted to one another.

Their friendship continued after Jesse went to college. In 1930, aged seventeen, he enrolled at Cleveland's East Technical High School. Jesse had never been interested in book work, and the Technical School was a place for learning job skills rather than academic study. It was a good place for Jesse to continue his passion for athletics.

In 1932 Minnie Ruth, now sixteen, told Jesse she was pregnant. At first, the Owens and Solomon families were furious with nineteen-year-old Jesse.

Surely these young people still had their own lives to sort out, before they would be ready for family responsibilities? Minnie Ruth left school and worked as a beautician in a shop called Wagner's. She stayed at her parents' house, where Jesse was no longer a welcome visitor. That summer she had a healthy baby daughter, and named her Gloria.

THE TECHNICAL STUDENT

At the Technical School, coach Edgar Weil soon realized he had a very talented student in his care. Jesse decided to concentrate on athletics rather than basketball or American football. He was very pleased when the school allowed Charles Riley to carry on coaching him. Jesse became the star of the school athletics team and was very popular with all the other students.

Jesse proudly shows his medals to his mother, in 1933.

Way out front –
Jesse Owens wins
the 220 yard
dash on 17 June
1933.

Top competition

Jesse was now seen as a rising star in the world of American athletics, a contender for serious international competition. In the summer of 1932 he even took part in the US **Olympic** trials, held at Northwestern University in Evanston, Illinois. He lost the 220 yards (201 metres) and 100 yards sprints to the great sprinter Ralph Metcalfe, who eventually became his close friend.

Jesse Owens was not selected for the US Olympic team which competed at the Los Angeles games that year. But he was now competing at the highest level and was learning all the time.

By 1933 he was being rated increasingly highly by the experts. In May of that year he powered his way to a leap of 24 ft 3 ½ ins (7 m 40 cm) in the long jump event at the Ohio State Interscholastic event.

Fame in Chicago

The following month saw the National Interscholastic Championships held at Chicago, Illinois. Jesse's electric performances had the radio commentators talking in superlatives; he jumped 24 ft 9 $^5/_8$ ins (7 m 54 cm); he equalled the world 100 yards record with a time of 9.4 seconds; and he ran the 220 yards in 20.7 seconds, a new world record.

Before his twentieth birthday, Jesse had achieved fame. Back in Cleveland, he was given a hero's welcome. He rode through the streets in a motor procession with his proud parents and coach Charles Riley. The city mayor, Ray Miller, congratulated him on his successes.

Mayor Ray Miller of Cleveland congratulates Jesse Owens on his record-breaking performance in Chicago.

Minnie Ruth was proud of Jesse, too. Her parents now agreed to allow him to visit their daughter and the baby. Jesse took a job at a filling station to bring in some money. The future was looking bright.

THE RECORD BREAKER

The next step for Jesse Owens was to join a university team. In the 1930s, the only route to the **Olympics** was via the university circuit as an amateur. American colleges would waive academic qualifications provided that the athletes could pass a basic entry test. No fewer than twenty-eight colleges offered Jesse a place as a student. His high school grades had not been very good, but he was tested and given the go-ahead for his first choice at a local university – Ohio State, in Columbus.

THE FRESHMAN

It was understood that Jesse would concentrate on athletics, but he did have to do academic work, too. He always found that hard, as he had never been given the right education. As the son of a poor African-American **sharecropper**, his teachers had never expected him to go to university.

Jesse's friends warned him to expect **racism** at college, and he found it. As an African-American, he was not allowed to live on **campus**. He could not share a car to an athletics meet with his white team mates or even use the same shower afterwards.

This was no surprise to Jesse. However, although he had known attitudes like these all his life it must

Segregation and discrimination against black people was widespread in the United States during the 1930s. This photo shows a segregated drinking fountain.

have been hard for the twenty-year-old **freshman** to be treated as inferior one minute and as the great athlete the next. But he did meet many kind people at college and was always good at making friends.

Thanks to the college, Jesse got a part-time job at the Ohio State House in Columbus – the place where the state debated and passed new laws. He worked as a lift operator and later as a page, carrying messages. He earned $3 a day and was known and liked by one and all.

Training for success

The university athletics coach was Larry Snyder, and he now took over where Charles Riley had left off. The programme of training was rigorous and well-planned. At the Amateur Athletic Union (AAU) meet in New York, in 1934, Jesse completed a long jump of 25 ft 3 ¼ ins (7 m 71 cm). He was now an athlete to contend with his greatest athletic rivals, Ralph Metcalfe and Eulace Peacock.

Pure magic

On 25 May 1935, Jesse Owens took to the track in Ann Arbor, Michigan, for the Big Ten Championship meet. Both he and Larry Snyder must have been anxious, for Jesse had hurt himself falling downstairs just a week before. There was a crowd of some 12,000 spectators.

At 3.15pm Jesse again equalled the world record for 100 yards, with a time of 9.4 seconds. At 3.25pm he jumped 26 ft 8 ¼ ins (8 m 12 cm) in the long jump, a world record that nobody else would beat for another twenty-five years. At 3.45pm he ran 220

Jesse's remarkable feats at Ann Arbor were followed by more athletic achievements.

yards in 20.3 seconds. This too was a world record and included the fastest ever 200 metres. At 4pm Jesse shattered another record, the 220-yard low hurdles, with a time of 22.6 seconds. Again, this included the fastest ever 200 metres. The events of that afternoon remain some of the most extraordinary athletic achievements ever witnessed.

COMING DOWN TO EARTH

Fame did not bring Jesse instant fortune, nor did it solve all his problems. The AAU was querying his amateur status as a competitor because of his paid job with the Ohio State House. The university complained that his academic work was not good enough. The strain was beginning to affect his running. At home in Cleveland, Minnie Ruth was worried that celebrity was taking Jesse away from her and Gloria. Minnie Ruth and Jesse decided to get married.

Jesse Owens and Minnie Ruth Solomon on their wedding day, 5 July 1935.

ANOTHER KIND OF RACE

Racism in sport
extended beyond
athletics. These
Chicago Giants
team members
played in an all
African-American
league. Baseball
was not integrated
until 1947.

Jesse Owens was clearly the amateur athlete of the year in 1935. However, the AAU gave the Sullivan Amateur Athlete of the Year award to a golfer called Lawson Little. It was a snub, and people wondered if the decision to exclude Jesse was based on **racism**.

RACISM AND SPORT

Why are African-American athletes superior to white ones? Whether that is true in the first place is debatable, but the question was raised in Jesse's day

Racism in sport extended beyond athletics. These Chicago Giants team members played in an all African-American league. Baseball was not integrated until 1947.

and it is still being asked today. Jesse Owens himself was examined by research scientists.

Then, people believed they could detect differences in the muscles, and today they talk about **genetics**. Most people fail to think of the obvious reason. If you are poor and the victim of **racial discrimination** in education and in the jobs market, then you need to win. Athletics and other sports offer a rare opportunity for wealth and recognition.

Sport and race

W Montague Cobb was a famous African-American who held the post of professor of anatomy at Howard University in Washington DC. He was fascinated by suggestions by racist athletics coaches that apparent African-American superiority on the track was the result of 'primitive' strength, of physical differences in the structure of the heel, or of other, social, causes. Cobb carried out a detailed examination of Jesse Owens. In 1936 he wrote in the *Journal of Health and Physical Education* that there was no significant difference in performance between blacks and whites and that there were no relevant physical differences. All that counted, he decided, was motivation and the surrounding influences with which the athlete had grown up.

THE NAZIS IN GERMANY

In Germany during the 1930s, **racism** was the official policy of the ruling **Nazi** Party. The country had been defeated in 1918, at the end of the First World War, and many Germans still felt bitter and humiliated. They were suffering from **economic** hardship, too.

The German leader, Adolf Hitler, saw political advantage in pinning the blame for the country's troubles on the **ethnic groups** he despised. He claimed that the northern Europeans belonged to a superior race that he called 'Aryan' and that other races, such as Jews and Africans, were sub-human.

Adolf Hitler preached his bizarre theories of 'racial purity' at huge rallies across Germany.

TO BOYCOTT THE GAMES?

When it was known that the 1936 **Olympic Games** were to be held in Nazi Germany, many Americans said that the USA should not send a team to compete, because of Nazi **persecution** of the Jews. The AAU had already voted to **boycott** the games back in 1933.

A banner unfurled on Nazi headquarters in 1935 reads: 'In defending myself against the Jew I strive in the work of the Lord.'

Some African-Americans believed that an Olympic boycott would be pure **hypocrisy**. The white sporting **establishment** in the United States was itself racist, they said, in the way it treated African-American athletes.

The US Olympic Committee decided to send a team. Sport, they argued, had nothing to do with politics. This was a line that Jesse Owens always supported. The Olympic trials were held in July 1936, in New York City. Jesse Owens won the 100 metres, 200 metres and the long jump. He was certain of his place in the team this time.

BEATING HITLER

The **Olympic** trials of 1936 were followed by an official dinner in New York City. Jesse Owens met the other American athletes who would be travelling to Berlin. He also met invited celebrities such as the baseball player George Herman 'Babe' Ruth (1895-1948), who in that same year was elected to the National Baseball Hall of Fame. At the dinner Ruth told Owens that the secret of success in any sport was to *know* that you were going to win. It was all down to self-confidence. Jesse took note.

It was the great age of ocean liners, and the US Olympic team travelled to Europe across the Atlantic on the luxurious *Manhattan*. The sea voyage lasted a week, and Jesse watched his diet and made sure he kept in training.

TO BERLIN

The *Manhattan* docked at Bremerhaven in northern Germany on 24 June 1936 and the US squad continued to the capital by train. They checked in at

Berlin's **Olympic village** along with the athletes of fifty-one other nations. Training now began in earnest, and Jesse's university coach Larry Snyder turned up to keep an eye on him and offer advice to the official US Olympic coaches.

IN THE PUBLIC EYE

An impressive new stadium, the Olympia-Stadion, had been built in Berlin's western suburbs to accommodate the expected daily crowds of about 70,000 to 110,000 spectators. The Berlin Olympics were the first to be televised. Powerful images of the games were recorded by the camera of Leni Riefenstahl, the German film-maker. Hitler commissioned Riefenstahl to make the official film of the games, *Olympische Spiele 1936*, also shown under the title *Olympiad*.

Leni Riefenstahl (centre) photographed while filming the 1936 Olympics.

PROPAGANDA

Adolf Hitler had intended the Games to be a showcase of **Nazi** Germany, a brilliant exercise in **propaganda**, designed to demonstrate to the world that the Aryan race was superior. Loyal Nazis with adoring faces lined the streets to watch Hitler drive by.

Hitler decided to show a liberal face to the world. Anti-Jewish posters were taken down, and some part-Jewish athletes were even allowed to represent Germany. Many visitors were fooled.

Some members of the American Olympic team takes a stroll through Berlin. Owens is third from the right.

THE FLAME IS LIT

The Games began on 1 August 1936 with the lighting of the **Olympic flame**, using a torch that had been relayed all the way from Greece, the ancient home of the Games. Hitler stood in the official box alongside other leading Nazis. They included Hermann Goering (1893-1946) and Joseph Goebbels (1897-1945). The latter was the evil genius who was Hitler's chief of propaganda.

The Olympic flame arrives at the packed Berlin stadium, beneath the swastika banners of Nazi Germany.

Hitler said that the Americans should be ashamed of themselves, allowing '**Negroes**' to win their medals for them. He also said that he would never shake hands with the African-American athletes, but in fact the International Olympic Committee (IOC) stopped the practice of each medal-winner being personally congratulated by Hitler, so the situation did not arise.

Powerful as Hitler was, he couldn't stop the German people warming to Jesse Owens. Everyone admired his charm, patience and easy manner.

It cannot have been an easy time for any of the athletes, let alone Jesse and the other African Americans representing the USA. Jesse did not dwell too much on the politics of it all. He had come to compete and that had to be his only thought if he was to succeed.

Take your marks!

The long-awaited Games had begun. First of all came the **heats**, the eliminating events. Jesse got off to a flying start with a 100 metre sprint in 10.3 seconds, matching his own record. In the next heat, managed 10.2 seconds, but with a following wind, which made it invalid as a record. The 100 metre semi-finals the next day were a creditable 10.4 seconds, and in the final Jesse stormed home with another 10.3. He had struck gold, and the crowd roared their appreciation.

> 'I was going to fly. I was going to stay up in the air forever.'
> Jesse Owens, on his record-breaking long jump

The following day saw the 200 metre heats, followed by the long jump. Jesse got through the former in record-breaking style, but ran into trouble with the latter. The German athlete Lutz Long gave Jesse useful advice about his run-up. They became friends immediately. The gold medal in the long jump finals was fought out between these two. The winner? Jesse Owens, with a record-breaking 26 ft 8 1/4 ins (8 m 13 cm).

Jesse Owens streaks to victory in the 200 metre race.

Hitler must have been increasingly frustrated. Not only had Lutz, his Aryan hero, lost, but Long had publicly shown his very real affection and admiration for an African American, a supposed 'sub-human' in Hitler's view.

The 200 metre final brought further humiliation for Hitler and the **Nazis**. At the end of it, Jesse was again number one, collecting the gold medal with an **Olympic** record of 20.7 seconds.

Flanked by a news reporter, Jesse Owens is congratulated by Swedish athlete Lennart Strandberg after winning the 100 metre sprint.

Jesse had finished his scheduled events, but the Olympic officials wanted him and Ralph Metcalfe to run in the 4 x 100 metre relay in place of the selected runners, Sam Stoller and Marty Glickman, who were Jewish. Jesse wanted them to run, but he was overruled.

'It seems to take an eternity, yet it is all over before you can think of what's happening.'
Jesse Owens, on the 100-metre sprint

Jesse Owens ran and again, with the help of his team mates, captured a gold medal for the United States with an outstanding time of 39.8 seconds.

ONE RACE TOO MANY

The Games were over and the crowds of international visitors and journalists left the leafy avenues of Berlin. The teams left, too. The stadium lay empty. Adolf Hitler's policies would soon lead to world war in Europe, and as a result there would be no more **Olympic Games** until 1948.

The AAU had arranged further meets across northern Europe for the US athletics team – in Dresden, Cologne, Prague, Bochum and at London's White City stadium. Stockholm was to be next, but Owens was exhausted. It was time to pack up and go home. Larry Snyder agreed, but the AAU was furious. Jesse was now the star attraction. Nevertheless, Jesse sailed from England for the USA on board the *Queen Mary*.

'As a **Negro**, I am proud of those black athletes who comported themselves so honourably in sportsmanship at Berlin.'
A letter from F V Harris to the British *Daily Telegraph* 1936

THE BERLIN LEGACY

Jesse Owens had put in one of the most remarkable Olympic performances of all time. He had also left the world with a series of unforgettable images, not of Aryan supremacy or of **Nazi** power, but of African-American excellence and beauty.

Photos of Jesse embracing Lutz Long seemed to symbolize the true Olympic spirit. They remained in the public imagination long after the German athlete was killed in the Second World War, which broke out just three years later. They even survived the city in which the games were held, for the Berlin that Jesse had come to know in the summer of 1936 was razed to the ground by bombing and fighting by the time Hitler's war ended, in 1945.

The German long jumper Lutz Long had not been afraid to show his friendship for Jesse Owens in front of the Nazi crowds.

THE HOMECOMING

When the *Queen Mary* sailed into harbour, Jesse Owens was one of the most famous men in the United States. He was welcomed back by his proud mother, Emma, and his jubilant wife, Minnie Ruth. There were impressive victory parades and public honours in Cleveland and in Columbus, Ohio.

Emma and Minnie Ruth welcome home the conquering hero.

Back in New York, Jesse met up with his team-mates from Berlin for the city's traditional **tickertape** parade. Paper showered down from Manhattan's skyscrapers like a blizzard of snow.

SOUR NOTES

Already, however, some parts of the victory were beginning to seem a little hollow. There were neither official congratulations from the office of US President F D Roosevelt, nor any invitation to meet the president at the White House.

The AAU, grudging as ever, suspended Jesse from membership for refusing to go to the Stockholm meet, even though Jesse had never signed up to it in the first place. In those days, amateur status was

> 'I came back to my native country and couldn't ride in front of the bus. I had to go to the back door ... I wasn't invited up to shake hands with Hitler, but I wasn't invited to the White House to shake hands with the President, either.'
>
> Jesse Owens, on his homecoming from Berlin

all-important to athletes and many other sporting stars. Amateur status was all very well if you were wealthy to start with, but for people from a poor background, like Jesse, an income was essential for survival.

A CHANGE OF DIRECTION

Jesse was offered advice by many people, including Ohio State coach Larry Snyder. He had a new friend, too, the African-American showbusiness personality and dancer, Bill 'Bojangles' Robinson, who met him on his return. Robinson introduced Jesse to his own **agent**, Marty Forkins. There was talk of big money, of film offers in Hollywood.

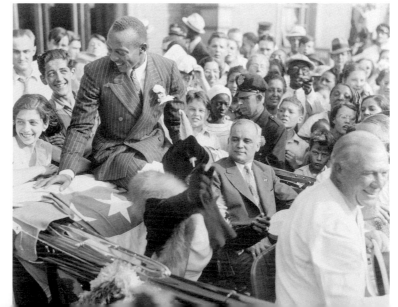

Crowds jostle to get a glimpse of America's most famous athlete during his victory parade.

> 'I've lost six pounds being circused and pushed all over Europe. I'm burned out and tired of being treated like a head of cattle.'
>
> Jesse Owens, on why he went professional

These deals were not on the scale successful athletes receive today, but they were considerable by the standards of the 1930s. Jesse's head was spinning.

Jesse decided to sign a contract with **agent** Marty Forkins. By doing so he knew he was finally breaking his links with the AAU. He did indeed have to quit the amateur athletics circuit, and tragically this proved to be the end of his career as a serious athlete.

Really, Jesse was burned out. He was exhausted by the tension of the Berlin **Olympics**, by the way in which African-American athletes were treated in the United States and by his new-found celebrity.

AN INSPIRATION

However, the story of Jesse Owens the athlete was far from over. Countless young athletes in the 1930s and 1940s were inspired by Jesse's example. One was Harrison Dillard, who watched Jesse's 1936 victory parade in Cleveland, wide-eyed in wonder. Dillard grew up to become a world-beating athlete between the years 1947 and 1952.

JESSE TAKES TO POLITICS

Jesse was no politician, but he did want to make things better for people. He turned out as a paid campaign speaker for Alf Landon, governor of the state of Kansas. Landon was on the progressive side of the conservative Republican Party. In 1936 Landon was challenging Roosevelt for the presidency. Jesse turned out to be a fluent and accomplished speaker in public, but Landon still lost the election.

Harrison Dillard hurdles in 1948. He was one of many youngsters who went on to follow the example of Jesse Owens.

THE SHOWMAN

Jesse Owens tried to organize a two-man race in Cuba on 26 December 1936. His opponent was to be the ace sprinter Conrado Rodrigues, but when the event was cancelled, Jesse agreed to run against a racehorse instead. He won and took the money. He went on to do more exhibitions like this. But they were unworthy of the great **Olympic** athlete who came to be billed, like some circus act, as 'The Ebony Antelope'.

Jesse Owens runs against a horse in 1948 – and wins.

BANDS, BASKETBALL AND BOXERS

Jesse was always the showman. In 1937 he got a contract as a bandleader from Bill 'Bojangles' Robinson, and went on tour. He cut a fine figure, but he wasn't really musical. He made good money for a few months. He set up touring basketball

Jesse Owens photographed with boxer Joe Louis in 1935.

teams, which performed exhibition matches across the USA. He ran, too, against leading baseball stars and even against the champion boxer, Joe Louis.

TIME TO RETHINK

Jesse was soon in serious financial difficulties. The big money that had been promised in 1936 never really materialized. He took a job as a playground director in Cleveland. The year 1938 saw him as boss of a dry-cleaning business, but it collapsed and left him $114,000 in debt.

Back in Europe, war finally broke out with **Nazi** Germany in 1939, although it was 1941 before the United States was drawn into the conflict.

These were troubled times for the Owens family, too. Jesse's mother died in March 1940, and his father died too, just six months later. Jesse and Minnie Ruth felt the loss keenly, but they were now parents to two more daughters of their own, Marlene (born in 1937) and Beverly (born in 1940). They found consolation in family life.

Jesse decided that it was time he had another crack at the Ohio State University degree he had abandoned before Berlin. He did some athletics coaching when he was back there, too. However, by 1941 Jesse had accepted that he was never going to complete his academic course and he left university.

WAR WORK

In late 1941 the United States entered the Second World War against Germany and Japan. Jesse now took on important war work with the Civilian Defense Office, organizing a national physical fitness programme. Later, the government offered him a job with the Ford Motor Company, which was at that time manufacturing vehicles for the war effort. Jesse became a **personnel officer**, dealing with African-American car workers in Detroit, Michigan. He negotiated with **trade unions**, and sorted out any social problems faced by the workers.

Jesse Owens continued to start up new businesses. He tried again with dry cleaning in 1954.

1945

In 1945, the Second World War came to an end. American, British, French and Russian troops occupied Germany. The long years of war had of course put an end to international athletics, including the **Olympic Games**. Jesse was still fit, but by now he was too old for top competition.

As the war ended, so did Jesse's contract with Ford. He was still the showman, and for a time worked as a disc jockey, with his own jazz show on the radio. With his restless energy, he was working at the same time on other plans.

Sport and politics

Although we may think that political rows and accusations of cheating are new in sport, they were common even in ancient Greece. In modern times, politics have cast their shadow over sport many times, not just at the Berlin Olympics. The Munich Olympics of 1972 saw members of the Israeli team taken hostage by Palestinian terrorists. Nine hostages, four terrorists and a policeman were killed in the shoot-out that followed. The Montreal Olympics of 1976 were **boycotted** by many black athletes in protest against the IOC's attitude to **racist** South Africa. The Moscow Olympics of 1980 were boycotted by the USA and West Germany because of outrage at the invasion and occupation of Afghanistan by the USSR. Australian Aborigines protested about racist laws in Australia at the Sydney Olympics in 2000.

MAN OF BUSINESS

Jesse Owens decided to found a **public relations** company after the war, and in 1946 he became head of sales for the Leo Rose Sporting Goods Company. He and his family moved to Chicago, Illinois in 1949.

Jesse Owens supported a number of conservative politicians. He campaigned for Richard Nixon in the 1960 presidential race.

THE TELEVISION AGE

The 1950s saw the new medium of television take over from radio. With the birth of television came the rapid growth of the advertising industry. Jesse took to it naturally and was soon advertising products on TV. His name and achievements were well remembered by the public. He took part in after-dinner speaking engagements for his **sponsors**, talking to groups of business people, religious organizations, sporting associations and so on. He was an outstanding success.

AN AMBASSADOR

Jesse always liked to emphasize that anyone could make it in the USA – just as he had. The message was one that found a ready response from his conservative audiences, and with Republican politicians such as

Dwight D Eisenhower, the wartime general who had led the Allied attack on Hitler between 1943 and 1945.

Eisenhower was US President between 1953 and 1961. This was a period of growing tension between the USA and its allies and the Russian communists of the Soviet Union – the start of a period known as the Cold War. Eisenhower sent Jesse as a 'goodwill ambassador' around the world – to India, Malaya and the Philippines. Here, as ever, he charmed and inspired many young people, talking about sport and the American way of life. He was described as a 'professional good example'.

ATHLETICS IN THE 1950S

Jesse's athletic achievements were not forgotten at home. In 1949 *Ebony*, an African–American magazine, voted Jesse the greatest African–American athlete of all time. The next year, the Associated Press voted him the greatest track and field athlete of the first half of the twentieth century.

Jesse devoted a lot of his time to the support of athletics in Chicago. He served as Secretary of the Illinois State Athletic Commission from 1952–55. He helped African–American youngsters at the Southside Boys' Club. In 1956, he organized a Junior Sports Jamboree for the Youth Commission in Illinois.

WHERE DO YOU STAND, BROTHER?

In the 1950s and 1960s, the tide of history again swept over Jesse Owens. Once again, the issue was race. African-Americans were pushing against the old injustices of **racial discrimination** and **segregation**, which still persisted in the south and in parts of the northern USA.

CIVIL RIGHTS?

A civil rights movement grew up under the inspired leadership of the African-American minister, Dr Martin Luther King Jnr. He preached non-violence and won over many liberal whites to his cause. In 1963, King organized a great march on the federal capital, Washington DC. It had a massive impact in the United States and around the world.

Civil rights marchers take to the streets of New York City. Jesse Owens had little sympathy with protest movements.

Jesse Owens offered no active support for the civil rights movement. He had never had a taste for political protest and did not find it in his middle age. He believed that African-Americans should achieve improved conditions by enterprise and hard work. Money brought power. It was a simplistic view, which did not reflect the reality of life for most African-American people living in the United States.

It was a conservative message, too, and these were not conservative times. Across the globe, African-American and white young people were trying to create a brave new world, with

Martin Luther King Jnr speaks of an end to racism, in June 1966.

new social attitudes, new music, new fashion – and a new sense of justice.

In 1968, Jesse Owens finally realized that he had lost touch with **grassroots** African-American thinking. In this year, Martin Luther King Jnr was shot dead by an assassin. In this year also, black America rose in protest, rioting and burning cities from Washington DC to Los Angeles. It was also the year of the Mexico City **Olympic Games**.

TO MEXICO CITY

Jesse was a fundraiser for the US Olympic Committee and he went to Mexico City unaware of the storm that was brewing. Most of the African-American athletes wished to make some form of protest. They wanted to air their bitterness at the way in which African-American athletes were still treated in the USA.

OLYMPIC PROTEST

They also wanted to join other African–American competitors in expressing outrage that the IOC President, Avery Brundage, had supported the campaign to allow South Africa to compete at the games. At that time, South Africa was ruled by a **racist** white government, which refused to grant the vote to citizens of black African or Asian descent.

Tommie Smith and John Carlos raise their fists and bow their heads at the Mexico City Olympics in 1968.

The world was astounded at the sight of Americans Tommie Smith and John Carlos, winners of gold and bronze medals in the 200 metres event, taking to the medals podium with their heads bowed during the playing of the US national anthem. The two athletes took off their shoes as a symbol of black poverty and raised their clenched and gloved fists in a salute normally associated with the **militant** Black Panther organization.

A row immediately erupted, in which the IOC demanded that the US athletes be sent home. The US Olympic Committee used Jesse Owens as **mediator**. Jesse tried to find a compromise, but failed and lost his temper in a furious argument.

BLAST AND COUNTERBLAST

Jesse expressed his anger over the incident in a book called *Blackthink*, co-written with journalist Paul Neimarck and published in 1970. It criticized the civil rights movement and said that if African-Americans failed, it was their own fault. Conservative Americans approved, but a torrent of criticism poured in from the African-American community.

Jesse was genuinely surprised by the reaction of his own people. He was persuaded to sit down and read a book called *Soul on Ice* by Eldridge Cleaver, an African-American writer and member of the Black Panther movement. As he read it, he realized how far he had come from the cotton fields of Alabama. For most African-Americans, poverty and discrimination were still a daily reality.

In the early 1970's, Jesse and Minnie Ruth moved to Arizona and he wrote another book called – with straightforward honesty – *I Have Changed*. In it, he agreed that militant protest has its place and its justification, provided it is non-violent.

FINAL HONOURS

By the end of the 1970s, Jesse Owens was at peace with his people and was respected in the United States and around the world. In 1972 his old university, Ohio State, had finally awarded him an honorary degree. In 1974 he was given the National Collegiate Athletic Association Theodore Roosevelt Award. In 1976 US President Gerald Ford awarded him the Presidential Medal of Freedom. And in 1979, US President Jimmy Carter gave him the Living Legend Award.

On 31 March 1980, James Cleveland 'Jesse' Owens died in Tucson, Arizona. The cause of death was lung cancer. Jesse had been smoking heavily for 35 years. Some 2000 people came to his funeral in Chicago. His coffin was draped with the **Olympic** flag.

The five-ringed flag of the Olympic movement is draped over the coffin of Jesse Owens.

In 1981, an annual Jesse Owens International Trophy was inaugurated for amateur athletes. And in 1983, the name of Jesse Owens was entered in the US Olympic Hall of Fame. At the opening of the 1984 Olympic Games in Los Angeles, California, Jesse's grand-daughter, Gina Hemphill, carried the torch. In 1990, Jesse was awarded the Congressional Gold Medal, which was collected by his widow, Minnie Ruth.

Gina Hemphill, Jesse's grand-daughter, enters the stadium at the 1984 Olympics.

IN MEMORY

Jesse Owens is still the only athlete ever to have beaten five world records in a single day – at Ann Arbor, Michigan, that afternoon in May 1935. His most memorable achievement, however, went beyond athletics. It was when he went to Berlin in the summer of 1936, and triumphed in the face of the **Nazis' racism**.

To Jesse Owens, the Olympic ideal was still a spiritual one, which went far beyond the world of politics and governments. His view was clear: 'The road to the Olympics ... leads to no city, no country. It goes far beyond ... Nazi Germany. The road to the Olympics leads, in the end, to the best within us.'

WHAT PEOPLE SAID ABOUT JESSE OWENS

'Jesse ran so fast I thought my stop-watch was out of order.'

Charles Riley, Jesse's coach 1927-33

'Jesse Owens listens and then he tries to put the suggestions into practice. He is so well co-ordinated that even a **radical** form change ... becomes part of his style after a very few practice sessions.'

Larry Snyder, Jesse's coach 1933-36

'[Owens] drew from the stands one of those sudden shouts, high-pitched and accentuated, which the Berlin crowd reserves for a specially popular win.'

London Morning Post, August 1936

'Do you really think that I will allow myself to be photographed shaking hands with a **Negro**?'

Adolf Hitler (as reported by Baldur von Schirach), August 1936

A painting of Jesse Owens in action dwarfs visitors to the 1996 Olympics in Atlanta.

'An American that all Americans should be proud of.'

Fiorello H La Guardia, New York City mayor and early anti-**Nazi** campaigner, 1936

'You were a child, a dark-skinned child, and you knew Jesse Owens before you even knew why. He had been a sprinter and a **broad-jumper**, that much you understood; but there was something more than just his speed that made black folk, even people who cared nothing about sports, swell their chests a little bit at the mention of his name. There was this one time when your house was full, loud with laughter, and a distinguished looking older man appeared on the television screen. "Isn't that Jesse?" somebody asked. "Hush, that's Jesse." And there was silence when Jesse Owens spoke.'

Phil Taylor in *Sports Illustrated*, 29 November 1999

JESSE OWENS – TIMELINE

1913   James Cleveland Owens is born in Oakville, Alabama

1922   The Owens family moves to Cleveland, Ohio. JC attends Bolton Elementary School, where he is given the name Jesse by mistake.

1927   Jesse is coached by Charles Riley at Fairmount Junior High School

1930   Jesse goes to Cleveland's East Technical High School

1932   Relationship with Minnie Ruth Solomon. Jesse's first daughter, Gloria, is born. Jesse fails to gain place in US Olympic team.

1933   National Interscholastic Meet: Jesse ties the world 100 yards record and breaks the 220 yards record. Jesse enrols at Ohio State University, works part-time at the Ohio State House.

1935   The Big Ten Championship at Ann Arbor, Michigan: Jesse achieves five world records in one afternoon. Jesse and Minnie Ruth get married.

1936   Member of the US Olympic team in Berlin. Jesse wins four gold medals and confounds the racists. Tickertape parade, New York City. Jesse quits amateur athletics. Campaigns for Alf Landon.

1937   Jesse does exhibition races, show-business appearances. His second daughter, Marlene, is born.

1938   Jesse's dry-cleaning business collapses

1940   Jesse's parents die. His third daughter, Beverly, is born. Jesse enrols at Ohio State University again.

1941	USA enters Second World War. Jesse runs national physical fitness campaign and goes on to become personnel officer for Ford Motors.
1945	End of the Second World War. Jesse starts up public relations company.
1949	Jesse and his family move to Chicago
1952	Jesse becomes Secretary of Illinois State Athletic Commission
1956	Organizes Junior Sports Jamboree
1963	Civil rights movement reaches peak
1968	Jesse Owens fails to defuse protest at the Mexico City Olympics
1970	Publishes *Blackthink*
1972	Publishes *I Have Changed*. Awarded honorary degree by Ohio State University.
1976	Awarded Presidential Medal of Freedom
1980	Jesse Owens dies in Tucson, Arizona
1981	Jesse Owens International Trophy inaugurated
1990	Awarded Congressional Gold Medal

GLOSSARY

agent someone who is paid a fee to find their clients work

boycott to refuse to take part or to buy, as a form of protest

broad-jump another term for long jump

campus the grounds of a university

civil war a war fought between citizens of the same country

colony a territory ruled or settled by another country

degenerate run down, morally corrupt

economy the way in which business, manufacture and employment are organized

elementary school in US, primary school for children aged between 5 and 11

establishment the existing organization or system

ethnic group people sharing common descent, language or culture

freshman a student in the first year of university

genetics the scientific study of genes, the units which programme the functions of all living things

grassroots the majority of people

heats the opening stages of an athletic event, used to select those athletes who will compete in the final

hypocrisy saying one thing but doing another

immigrant someone who moves from one country to live in another one

integrated a situation, for example a school or club, where black and white people mix together

mediator a go-between

militant politically aggressive

native home-born, original to the region

Nazi a member of the National Socialist German Workers' Party, founded after the First World War. Its politics were racist, nationalistic and aggressive.

Negro a word formerly used to describe a black person; the term is now generally considered to be offensive

Olympic Games the world's chief international sports competition, held in different cities around the world every four years

Olympic flame a flame symbolizing the Olympic spirit, lit by a torch at the beginning of the games

Olympic village accommodation used by athletes and their coaches during the Olympic Games

persecution harassment or cruelty inflicted upon a person or group of people

personnel officer somebody who deals with the people employed by a firm, paying their wages, processing their job applications, etc

pneumonia a disease of the lungs

propaganda information, true or false, put out to persuade people of a political argument

public relations ('PR') the promotion of goodwill among the public by a company or other organization

racial discrimination favouring people from one ethnic group over another

racism a belief in the division of humanity along racial lines

radical ground-breaking

segregated set apart, divided on racial lines

sharecropper a tenant farmer who has to pay a share of the crop he grows as rent

slave someone who is deprived of freedom to be bought and sold for forced labour

sponsor someone who pays people for their support

swastika an ancient symbol of well-being, chosen by the Nazis as an emblem of the so-called Aryan race

tickertape a ribbon of white paper on which news reports were once printed out. It used to be showered on to passing parades from New York City offices. Today, shredded paper is used instead.

trade union an association of workers which aims to protect working conditions and wages

INDEX